D1535879

Guinea Pigs

Tamra
Orr

PURPLE TOAD
PUBLISHING

P.O. Box 631
Kennett Square, Pennsylvania 19348
www.purpletoadpublishing.com

PURPLE TOAD
PUBLISHING

Copyright © 2014 by Purple Toad Publishing, Inc. All rights reserved. No part of this book may be reproduced without written permission from the publisher. Printed and bound in the United States of America.

Printing   1   2   3   4   5   6   7   8   9

A TOMMY TIGER book

WHAT ARE THEY SAYING?

Birds
Cats
Dogs
Guinea Pigs
Horses

Publisher's Congress-in-Publication Data
Orr, Tamra
   What Are They Saying: Guinea Pigs / Tamra Orr
      p. cm. — (What are they saying?)
Includes bibliographic references and index.
ISBN: 978-1-62469-030-3 (library bound)
1. Guinea pigs as pets – Juvenile literature.   I. Title.
  SF459.G9 2013
  636.93592 — dc23

                                                                    2013936065

eBook ISBN: 9781624690310

ABOUT THE AUTHOR: Tamra Orr is author of more than 350 books for readers of all ages. She lives in Oregon with three kids, one husband, one cat and one dog. She has never had her own guinea pig, but lived next door to two and took every chance to go over and pet them.

PUBLISHER'S NOTE: The data in this book has been researched in depth, and to the best of our knowledge is factual. Although every measure has been taken to give an accurate account, Purple Toad Publishing makes no warranty of the accuracy of the information and is not liable for damages caused by inaccuracies.

Printed by Lake Book Manufacturing, Chicago, IL

WHAT ARE THEY SAYING?

Guinea Pigs

A Missing Boy

I was sad. The little boy had not come to play with me all day. That was not like him. In the mornings, he always came to see me. He would give me water. He would fill up my food bowl. Some days he even gave me a treat like a leaf of lettuce or a piece of cucumber.

He did not do any of that today.

I let out a squeal. I waited. The boy knew that when I made that noise, it meant come and play with me. I waited longer. He still did not come, so I squealed louder. I was letting him know I was lonely.

It did not work. Now I started to chirp to say I was upset. No one came. I was not sure what to do. I went and hid inside a pile of hay and wood shavings. It was where I felt safe until my boy came to see me.

No one is quite sure how guinea pigs got their name. The animals do not come from New Guinea. They are not a type of pig. They are a type of rodent, like a mouse, rat, or hamster.

Some think the name came from how much it once cost to buy the animal in England— one guinea.

The front door slammed. People were talking loudly. My ears can hear sounds better than people, cats, and dogs. The loud noises hurt me. It was scary.

I sat still and did not move. Just then the little boy came into the room. He had his hands behind his back. I was so glad to see him! "Be quiet!" he said to the people. "You know it scares Cody when we yell."

The loud noises stopped. Then I heard something new. What was it? It sounded like the chirp I made when I was upset. Where was it coming from? The little boy smiled at me. He showed me what he had in his hands. It was another guinea pig! I began to squeal and grunt to say I was happy.

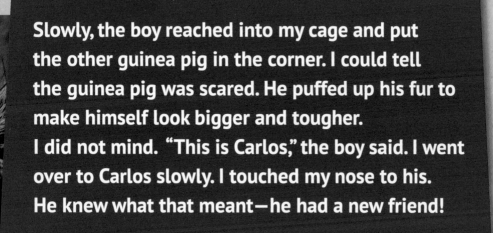

Slowly, the boy reached into my cage and put the other guinea pig in the corner. I could tell the guinea pig was scared. He puffed up his fur to make himself look bigger and tougher.
I did not mind. "This is Carlos," the boy said. I went over to Carlos slowly. I touched my nose to his. He knew what that meant—he had a new friend!

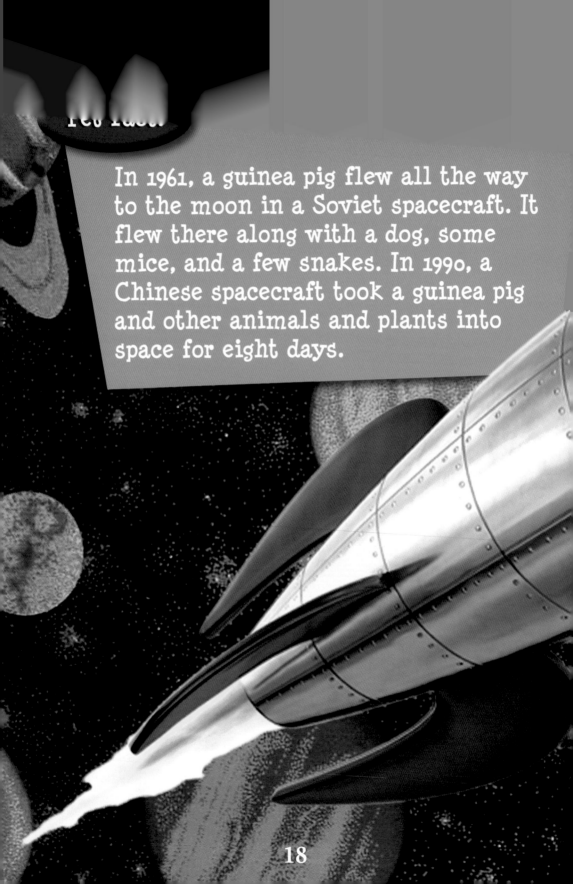

Fact Fact!

In 1961, a guinea pig flew all the way to the moon in a Soviet spacecraft. It flew there along with a dog, some mice, and a few snakes. In 1990, a Chinese spacecraft took a guinea pig and other animals and plants into space for eight days.

Out to
Play

Guinea pigs are not meant to live alone. Long ago, in the wild, we lived in herds. So many animals hunted us that we had to live together in order to stay safe.

The little boy came into the room and carefully picked me up. He held one hand under me. He put the other on top. I cooed and purred to show I liked it.

He took me outside and put me in the play area. It had a fence so other animals could not get in, and we could not get out. It had toys like a cardboard box, a grocery bag, a paper cup, and a straw basket.

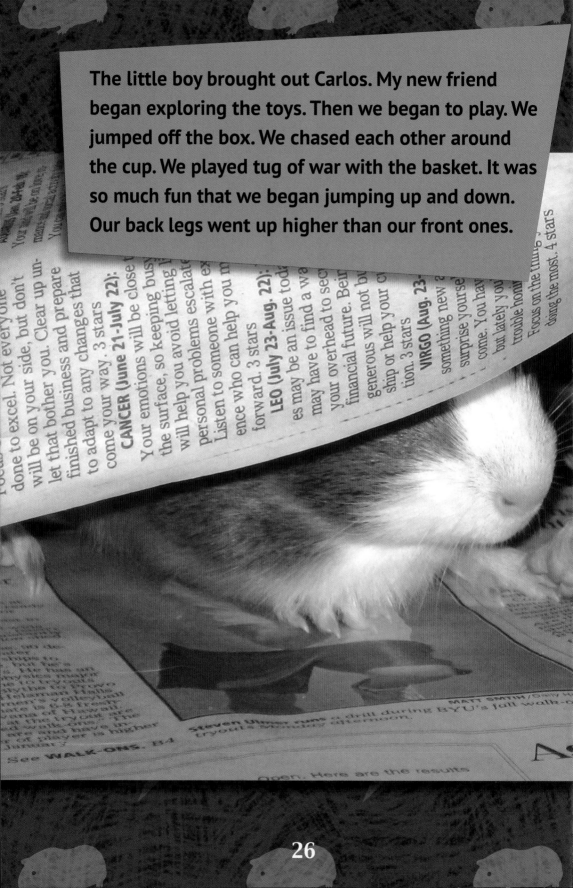

The little boy brought out Carlos. My new friend began exploring the toys. Then we began to play. We jumped off the box. We chased each other around the cup. We played tug of war with the basket. It was so much fun that we began jumping up and down. Our back legs went up higher than our front ones.

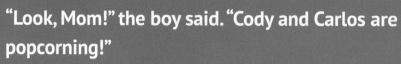

"Look, Mom!" the boy said. "Cody and Carlos are popcorning!"
The boy was right. We were doing the guinea pig dance of happiness. We had food, water, toys, a home—and now we each had a friend.

Pet Fact:

When you have guinea pigs, it is best to have two boars (males) or two sows (females), than one of each because they get along the best that way. If you have one boy and one girl, you may also end up with more guinea pigs than you want!

Books

Alderton, David. *How to Look After Your Guinea Pig: A Practical Guide to Caring for Your Pet.* Armadillo, 2012.

Goodbody, Slim. *Slim Goodbody's Inside Guide to Guinea Pigs.* Gareth Stevens, 2008.

Pavia, Audrey. *Guinea Pig: Your Happy Healthy Pet.* Howell Book House, 2005.

Rayner, Matthew. *Guinea Pig.* Gareth Stevens, 2008.

Works Consulted

Birmelin, Immanuel. *Guinea Pigs: A Complete Pet Owner's Manual.* Barron's Educational Series, 2008.

Noah, Hilary. "The Domestic Guinea Pig," Tree of Life. http://tolweb.org/treehouses/?treehouse_id=4713

Pavia, Audrey. *Guinea Pig: Your Happy Healthy Pet.* Howell Book House, 2005.

Unknown. "Guinea Pig Sounds of Communication." Expert Guinea Pig Care. http://www.expertguineapigcare.com/guinea-pig-sounds/

Unknown. "Understanding your Pet Guinea Pig: A Guide to Behavioral Patterns." Hartz. http://www.hartz.com/Small_Animals/Health_and_Nutrition/Health/Understanding_Your_Pet_Guinea_Pig_A_Guide_to_Behavioral_Patterns.aspx

On the Internet

BCSPCA: Pet Care for Guinea Pigs http://www.spca.bc.ca/youth/about-animals/pet-care/guinea-pig-care-for-kids.html

Blue Cross for Pets—Guinea Pig Care http://jackiesguineapiggies.com/beforeadoptingaguineapig.html

Guinea Pig Care Charts http://www.kidpointz.com/printable-charts/pet-care-charts/guinea-pig

How to Care for Gerbils, Hamsters, and Guinea Pigs http://www.hellokids.com/c_20670/reading-online/reports/animal-reports-for-kids/pet-reports-for-kids/how-to-care-for-gerbils-hamsters-and-guinea-pigs

Piggie Care http://jackiesguineapiggies.com/beforeadoptingaguineapig.html

GLOSSARY

boars—Male guinea pigs.
herds—Groups of animals.
popcorning—Jumping up and down with hind legs raised.

rodent—Species of animals that include mice and rats.
sows—Female guinea pigs.

INDEX

PHOTO CREDITS: Cover and all photos—cc-by-sa-2.0. Every measure has been taken to find all copyright holders of material used in this book. In the event any mistakes or omissions have happened within, attempts to correct them will be made in future editions of the book.

GEORGE H. & ELLA M.
RODGERS MEMORIAL LIBRARY
194 DERRY ROAD
HUDSON, NH 03051